"An epic work. Apart fr[...] has now become a majo[...] of snappy ironic dialogu[...] painful poetry."

—CBC Radio

"The art of theatre doesn't get much better than this."
—*The Edmonton Sun*

"Burkett's status as a true theatre renegade is confirmed with *Provenance*."
—*The Edmonton Journal*

"To be captivated by Burkett, with or without puppets, you need simply to obey the show's opening words: "Follow my voice".... It's a remarkably fecund piece of work."
—*The Financial Times*, London

"*Provenance* really is poetry of the puppets. Uniquely brilliant."
—*Manchester Evening News*, Manchester

"Burkett's profound puppetry in *Provenance*, his latest work of genius, is so astonishing that it beggars belief just one person creates so complex an evening of theatre."
—*The Vancouver Sun*

"*Provenance* is exquisite and Burkett at his most vulnerable, courageous best."
—*The Vancouver Courier*

"*Provenance* is an intelligent, generous work of art."
—*The Georgia Straight*, Vancouver

"Burkett's writing at its wittiest and most evocative."
—*Fast Forward*, Calgary

"It is—and excuse the cliché—theatre magic."
—*The Globe and Mail*

"*Provenance* not only peers intently into the mirror to look at human nature but strips its propensity for camouflage and pretence bare."
—*Sydney Morning Herald*, Australia

"In *Provenance* Ronnie Burkett once again offers us a truly remarkable theatrical experience with enormous impact."
—*The Age*, Australia

PROVENANCE

Provenance

written and performed by

Ronnie Burkett

Playwrights Canada Press
Toronto • Canada

Provenance © Copyright 2005 Ronnie Burkett
The moral rights of the author are asserted.

Playwrights Canada Press
215 Spadina Avenue, Suite 230, Toronto, Ontario CANADA M5T 2C7
416-703-0013   fax 416-408-3402
orders@playwrightscanada.com • www.playwrightscanada.com

CAUTION: This play is fully protected under the copyright laws of Canada and all other countries of The Copyright Union, and is subject to royalty. Changes to the script are expressly forbidden without the prior written permission of the author. Rights to produce, film, or record, in whole or in part, in any medium or any language, by any group, amateur or professional, are retained by the author. For production rights, contact Playwrights Canada Press at the above address.

No part of this book, covered by the copyright hereon, may be reproduced or used in any form or by any means—graphic, electronic or mechanical—without the prior written permission of the publisher except for excerpts in a review. Any request for photocopying, recording, taping or information storage and retrieval systems of any part of this book shall be directed in writing to Access Copyright, 1 Yonge Street, Suite 1900, Toronto, Ontario CANADA M5E 1E5 416-868-1620.

Playwrights Canada Press acknowledges the financial support of the Canadian taxpayer through the Government of Canada Book Publishing Industry Development Programme (BPIDP) for our publishing activities.
We also acknowledge the Canadian and Ontario taxpayers through the Canada Council for the Arts and the Ontario Arts Council.

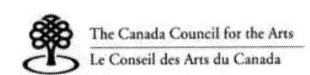

Cover photo by Trudie Lee.
Production editing & cover design: JLArt

Library and Archives Canada Cataloguing in Publication

Burkett, Ronnie, 1957-
          Provenance / written and performed by Ronnie Burkett.

A play.
ISBN 0-88754-788-5

          I. Title.

PS8553.U639P76 2005   C812'.6   C2005-901981-6

First edition: April 2005.
Printed and bound by AGMV at Quebec, Canada.

All production photographs in the book and on the cover by Trudie Lee.

For David Ross and Gemma Smith

Notes on Staging

The set for *Provenance* is a stylised bar/parlour intended to suggest a brothel. The decor is loosely inspired by Art Nouveau, and as such, the set is curvilinear and ornamental. It consists of a two-level deck; the downstage main acting area one foot above stage floor and an upstage level two feet above the stage. These are connected by ramps on either side of the set. Downstage left and right are puppet-scale stair units connecting to the ramps, used by marionettes for entrance into the brothel.

The downstage acting deck is oval and painted to resemble a swirling mosaic floor. A large bar-like unit sits upstage centre of this deck. This serves not only as a background for the main marionette action, but also as a counter for the upstage manipulation of table-top figures and jointed dolls. The front of the bar unit is painted to suggest an inlaid wood design depicting a forest. At the bottom of this detail are cutouts faced with pebbled clear acrylic which are backlit during the show to suggest the lights of Paris and later, a frozen pond.

The ramps and the upstage deck are painted gloss red. Sitting at the furthest upstage point and running the full width of the set are nine tall cabinets to house the seventeen marionettes used during the performance. The height of these cabinets varies and creates a wave across the upstage of the set. The fronts are also curved, both inward and out. They are painted in the same style as the bar front, depicting the inlaid wood forest scene. Each door has cutouts backed with acrylic "glass."

Set slightly off-centre between the cabinets is a large painting. It depicts a young man, nude save for green silk stockings, leaning against a tree. Wrapping around both the figure and the tree is a swan. The background and border are decorative in a post-Secessionist style.

A variety of puppet types are used in the performance. In addition to the marionettes in the cabinets, the underside of the bar unit serves as "offstage" storage for fully-jointed table-top figures, the dolls of child Leda and Tender, and handpuppets of Plato, Herschel and Maybelline. A small shelf sits below the upstage painting and is used for the figure of Pity on a platter and to hold the headrigs. These are headband contraptions holding various character heads directly in front of Ronnie's face. Various characters are represented by a number of figures and types. Leda is shown at four different ages, represented by four marionettes, one headrig, a jointed doll and two table-top figures. Pity is the same age, however due to costume changes, she is represented by five marionettes, a headrig, a jointed doll and a table-top figure.

Stage directions herein are kept to a minimum. The play is performed solely by Ronnie Burkett, and reference to him is throughout the staging directions. Standard staging abbreviations are used in this text, USC meaning "upstage centre", SL meaning "stage left" and so on. Cathy Nosaty's score and Bill Williams' lighting design are integral to the overall design and performance, although lighting and sound notes within this text are referred to only when necessary to the reading.

The play is performed without an interval, with a running time of approximately 2:06.

Production Information

Provenance premiered at Theatre Network in Edmonton, Alberta in October 2003. Subsequent runs include The Vancouver East Cultural Centre (Vancouver, British Columbia), CanStage (Toronto, Ontario), Alberta Theatre Projects (Calgary, Alberta), BITE:04, The Barbican Centre (London, UK), queerupnorth (Manchester, UK), Wiener Festwochen (Vienna, Austria), Melbourne International Arts Festival (Melbourne, Australia), Queensland Performing Arts Centre (Brisbane, Australia), Great Canadian Theatre Company (Ottawa, Ontario), Manitoba Theatre Centre (Winnipeg, Manitoba), Södra Teatern (Stockholm, Sweden), Kampnagel (Hamburg, Germany), The Brighton Festival (Brighton, UK).

Produced by Rink-A-Dink Inc./Ronnie Burkett Theatre of Marionettes.

Provenance is a co-production with BITE (London, UK), CanStage (Toronto, Canada), Melbourne International Arts Festival (Melbourne, Australia), queerupnorth (Manchester, UK) and Wiener Festwochen (Vienna, Austria).

Provenance was initiated during the CanStage Play Creation group, 2002. Ronnie Burkett's participation as the CanStage Playwright in Residence was made possible by a Senior Artist Grant from The Canada Council for the Arts.

Written and Performed by Ronnie Burkett
Music and Sound Design by Cathy Nosaty
Lighting Design by Bill Williams
Stage Managed by Angie Jones
Artistic Associate/Production Manager: Terri Gillis
Associate Producer: John Lambert
Dramaturge: Iris Turcott
Director of Lighting: Kevin Humphrey
Director of Sound/Technical Director: Shanna Miller
Marionettes, Costumes and Set Designed by Ronnie Burkett

Puppet Studio

Marionettes sculpted and carved by Ronnie Burkett
Assistant Designer/Shop Foreman: Dina Meschkuleit
Additional Sculpture: Angela Talbot, Noreen Young, Jo-Ellen Trilling, Dina Meschkuleit, Kim Crossley
Studio Team: Darren Pickering, Candace Russell, Wini Mertens, Emma Dalziel
Marionette Controls: Luman Coad, Frank Meschkuleit, Wulf
Stringing: Charleen Wilson
Studio Mascots/Supervisors: Charlie and Daisy

COSTUMES
Built by Kim Crossley
Assisted by Elizabeth Copeman, June Crossley, Casey Falardeau, Trish McNally, Dina Meschkuleit and Katri Tahvanainen

SET CONSTRUCTION
Master Carpenter: Martin Herbert
Carpenters: Carl Eric Lindgren, Terri Gillis
Set Assistance: Werner Karson and Barb Pierce

SCENIC PAINTING
Head Scenic Artist: Jennifer Hedge
Scenic Painter: Corrine Dickson
Scenic Painter: Kim Stewart

PROPS
Heather Kent, Wulf
Plato's rollerskates made by Jeff deBoer

"Tender" painted by Ronnie Burkett
Digital graphic rendering by John Alcorn

Special Thanks

Tanja Farman, John Malpass, Robyn Archer, Marie Zimmermann, Louise Jeffreys, Toni Racklin, Martin Bragg, Bonnie Green, Bradley Moss, University of Calgary Theatre Services, Alberta College of Art & Design, Green Fools Theatre Society and everyone at Crump Manor, Theatre Network, Jamie Hopkings, Mark Korven, Gina Puntil, Frank Meschkuleit, John Alcorn, Ray and Eileen Burkett, Trudie Lee Photography, Trish Leeper, Jason Hopley, Denise Clarke, Melissa Waddell

Characters

PITY BEANE, a Canadian art academic
LEDA OTENREATH, the madam of a Viennese brothel
TENDER, a young man in a painting
HERSCHEL FLECHTHEIM, an elderly American
VESPA POOPERMANN, manageress of the brothel
PLATO, the brothel monkey
DOOLEY OTENREATH, Leda's husband
AUNTIE SARI, Leda's imaginary aunt, and a cow
MR. HIRO, a Japanese businessman
MUSETTE, a lady of the brothel
JOHANNA, a lady of the brothel
IRIS, a lady of the brothel
MISS MAYBELLINE, a lady of the brothel

PROVENANCE

Pre-set LX fades as Ronnie enters. He stands CS.

RONNIE Follow my voice.

The painting of TENDER, USC, glows as he continues.

There were trees in the background
Rows of trees, not big but many
Each delicate in their creamy white stance
Thin-skinned bark draped like crepe
There were trees in the background
Rows of them, a fortress of interlocked fingers
A fine fence, gently holding back all intrusion
There were trees in the background
Filtering lace patterned light
Like snowflakes cut from paper
Skin whiter than ever before
Lace, snowflakes, trees
One would barely notice the blood at all

A train whistle blows. Light up on LEDA. She is a grand woman, elegant and elderly.

LEDA I spend my days in vain reflection
Dim the light and the mirror is kind
If you're blind
But never, forever, on closer inspection
Do I see the sight I have in mind

She removes her dark glasses.

Well, never mind. When one's nose is pressed against the glass, you're bound to catch a glimpse of what those on the other side see. But it's a backward resemblance, nevertheless. Like a painting, viewed upon completion. The final coat of varnish protecting the surface, the unknown layers of glaze, the first coal smudge upon the canvas. That primal line, tentative or bold, is the soul of art. The rest, veneer, added with time. And why shouldn't it be so? But what of the art of the soul? God himself has it backwards. We should be born old and dumb, finding our truth as we grow into youth. Body and mind growing together in knowing and strength. But no. God doesn't want us that strong. We see ourselves fully reflected only when the mirror cracks.

Light up on PITY. She is in her early 20s, and although her clothing is a funky blend of retro and practical (50s day dress and swing coat with brown Blundstone boots), PITY is nevertheless clearly and painfully plain.

PITY Catalogued wishes mark endless lists
Life as a dream on an empty purse
What is worse
Than to long for a song that can never exist
Or a kiss, that alone, I rehearse

My dad's boyfriend said there were three important things to remember. One, always take the Tylenol before doing poppers. Two, practice sincerity in front of the mirror, you never know when you'll need it. And three, if you leave a man, take the copper pots and your good knives. Otherwise, you'll never see them again. Not in this life. Not the life you're leaving. "Appliances can be replaced" he would tell me, "but honey, you need your knives." He wasn't a nice man, which is not to say that he was bad. Uncle Boyfriend was just different. I guess that's why he left.

TENDER is a beautiful young man. He is dressed in a simple cheap suit, the type found in a mail order catalogue in the early part of the 20th Century.

TENDER Given a gun and a foreign kilt
A boy man just beginning to shave
Go be brave
In the stench of the trench where your blood will be spilt
With burnt offerings sharing your grave

I ran twice. The first time, I took the train. It took me, away from home. The second time, I was trained not to run, but I had to. I had no choice. I was the train. Heart pounding, breath short, everything on the sidelines just a blur. It's as though everything around you were in motion, and you're just standing still. Both times I ran, and barely moved a muscle.

LEDA When I was a little girl, the animals talked. Auntie Sari, always a cow. A grand bovine woman with hooves stuffed into moss green pumps. The cook, Anna, a bleating old

	sheep, soft tufts of mad wool bursting from her cap. Daddy, the serious snouted pig, digging through his dealings as if they were truffles, his dark dim eyes serious and unforgiving. And Mummy, the show dog. Sleek and elegant, erect and alert, obeying every command her breeding demanded. The pig and the purebred, that's where I came from.
PITY	I travelled the world as a child, and never once left home. Uncle Boyfriend cooked, and every year chose a new country to master. At age ten, I was given books on the Orient, Chinese lanterns hung above my bed and Barbie wore a kimono. That was stir-fry year, and I thought we'd all be found murdered in our sleep if he didn't perfect sticky rice. At eleven and twelve it was Italian, but I didn't dare leave for school without saying "Ciao." I was a willing student in his global game, but my participation never got high marks. "Pity" he would say to me, "you're too bookish. You analyze everything. Less Bette Davis and more Joan Crawford. Feel it girl! You've got to push your brain down to your cunt." To date, I've managed to keep the two quite separate.
TENDER	I was fifteen years old, and I looked it. They allowed me to run and lie and leave. That first train took me away from a tiny still-life in a vast ocean of wheat, and rolled across Canada until there was no more land. Just the ocean. I had seen pirate battles waged upon it in my Boy's Own Companions, but I was not prepared for the beauty of her. I had to cross over this liquid prairie. To kill. To die. Beauty washed me, with salt in every wound. They expected me to walk on water.
LEDA	My nanny Marie raised me better than an English girl should be. She was beautiful, in that way that only French women have, and not even the hint of a slight moustache could detract from her appeal. In fact, it added to her aura I think, for surely her goodnight kisses to my young face conditioned me to swoon in later years whenever a man's facial hair would brush my cheek, scratch my breast or tickle my fancy. Marie is the only one who was not an animal. She was real and human and beautiful. I was her

	pet. My hair was strawberry coloured, and she called me her little pink puppy. No man could ever say anything so lovely as that. So I never kissed them back.
PITY	No boy in school was like him. He lived in the library, sleeping in a book. And every time I stole away to him, opening the page with hot teenage girl fingers, there he was. Awake and looking at me. I kissed him for the first time, there in the stacks. And now I am finally travelling to him. My beauty. I'm going to see him at last, with all his glazed layers revealing his infinite depth. I'm going to kiss him for real, and finally, lose my brain.
TENDER	I have been kissed once. In flesh. I have been kissed a thousand times, strange lips pressing against some two

	dimensional version of what I am. What do they want? What do they expect? I have no voice but theirs. Yet, they kiss me and wait for an answer that will never be spoken. I cannot love them back.
LEDA	I kissed beauty on the lips. Tender, for a moment. The swan-like down of youth that brushed my lips but once, now watches them lie forever. My purgatory is a heart that beats on borrowed breath. Beauty lives within me, but there is no dreaming when still. It lives, fully and real in front of me, pressing against my chest with every step I make. I want to stand still. I can't run anymore.
	A train whistle blows, followed by the sound of steam as if a train were pulling into a station. Light on TENDER only.
TENDER	There were trees in the background, unseen now I know they are there, no need to look back I am captured at last, gazing out beyond the past The landscape is full, of trees and me But the canvas is still. Still life. Still blank. The taut stretched fabric of my skin empty Save for snowflake light and blood It might be beautiful, this With only one view, that's all there is to see There were trees in the background Me in the foreground But all I see is you Seeing nothing, looking at me
	He disappears. Scene shift, rain SFX. PITY is at the foot of the stairs into the brothel. SFX of a bell. VESPA appears at the top of the stairs.
VESPA	If you're an American, go away. You are not welcome here.
PITY	No, no, no. I'm from Canada.
VESPA	Same thing.
PITY	You Germans are so kind.
VESPA	I'm Austrian.
PITY	Same thing. *Sig heil, Fraulein*!

VESPA	*Touché*, my dear. I don't know whether to slap or embrace you.
PITY	Neither, please. I'm Canadian, we prefer not to be touched at all.
VESPA	Welcome to Vienna. You'll fit right in.
PITY	May I come in?
VESPA	That depends.
PITY	On what?

VESPA	On what you want.
PITY	I want to get out of the rain.
VESPA	Stupid tourist. Who would travel in Europe without an umbrella?
PITY	I have an umbrella, it's in my bag.
VESPA	Then use it.
PITY	I can't. It's wet, still.
VESPA	That's what umbrellas are for!
PITY	No, it's wet from Paris. See, I was there, before I came here. And it rained so much, but I didn't mind. It seemed… right. Right as rain. And on the train, coming here, I took it out of my bag and I could smell it still. Paris. A real memory.
VESPA	And Parisian rain is better than Vienna's? It's all the same, *ja*? We've got the Euro now.
PITY	No, not better, just Paris. I plan to have a different memory of Vienna.
VESPA	Then go eat some torte, see a Klimt, tour a palace, take the tram around the Ringstrasse, eat Wiener Schnitzel until you explode! I don't care! Just leave me alone. Well, what are you waiting for? I said go away.
PITY	I won't. I'm expected here. I have an appointment.
VESPA	*Ja*, I doubt it. We don't cater to women. The Madam is very particular about which specialties she allows. Try Frau Wieser down the street. Her girls will do anything.
PITY	No, Mr. Flechtheim told me to meet him here.
VESPA	You know Herschel?
PITY	Well, not exactly. We corresponded, and he told me to meet him at this address. Please let me in, I'm soaked to the bone. I don't want to get sick.
VESPA	*Ja*, but then you could take a romantic European illness home with you.

PITY rings the bell.

	What are you doing?
PITY	Look, I've come a long way and I will not be turned back now.
	She rings the bell again.
VESPA	Stop that. You'll wake The Madam.
PITY	I've no idea who the Madam is, but clearly she's in charge and I would like to speak to her.
	She rings the bell again.
VESPA	I'm in charge. I decide who gets in and who doesn't.
	PITY rings the bell again.
	Enough!
PITY	I am to meet Mr. Herschel Flechtheim at this address. Now, will you let me in, you mannish shrew?
VESPA	You little American bitch!
PITY	Canadian bitch, thank you very much. Now will you let me in, or do I have to kick this door in and you down with it?
VESPA	You wouldn't dare!
PITY	Lady, I was raised by two gay men. You have no idea what this bitch is capable of. Well? May I enter, gentle woman? Or do I have to open a fresh can of Liza and Judy's whoop-ass?
VESPA	Don't drip on anything.
	VESPA steps aside, allowing PITY to enter.
	Tourists.
	Music and lights reveal the brothel. PITY stands in the centre of the room taking it in.
PITY	Vienna!
VESPA	*Willkommen zum Affenkaffee,* or, as the Yankee doodles call it, The Monkey Bar.
PITY	Uncle Boyfriend would love this place.

VESPA	Uncle Boyfriend?
PITY	He's my step-father. I swear he'd shit himself if he saw this room.
VESPA	*Ja*, well, good thing for the floor he's not here. Wait, I'll find Mr. Flechtheim. Your name, *fraulein*?
PITY	I'm Pity. Pity Beane.
VESPA	Of course you are.
PITY	And you?
VESPA	What?
PITY	Your name?
VESPA	I didn't say it.
PITY	That's why I'm asking.
VESPA	Poopermann. Vespa Poopermann.
PITY	Of course you are.
VESPA	You can hang your coat in here, Fraulein Beane.

> VESPA *exits, hung in a cabinet. The marionette of* PITY *is put into the cabinet as well, as Ronnie exchanges her for another version. It is* PITY *in the same costume, without the coat.* PLATO *the monkey enters on roller skates. He wears a little tuxedo and a fez. He sings.*

Ah Beauty

PLATO	Ah beauty! Ah beauty! Will you light upon my heart And if thou art, let my soul be awed Ah beauty! Settle here and steal my gaze Nestle close and spend your days And waken me to God

Oh beauty! Oh beauty!
Take my hand and lead me there
And show me where there's no blindness
Oh beauty!
Help to halt my backward pace
Turn me toward the radiant grace
Heaven's kiss of kindness

The song ends and PLATO exits. HERSCHEL enters.

HERSCHEL   I see you've met Plato.

PITY   Hello. Plato?

HERSCHEL   The joint was named in his honour. Herschel Flechtheim. You must be Miss Beane, from Canada.

PITY   Yes, Pity Beane.

HERSCHEL   Well, that's an interesting name, my dear. Tell me, is it short for something else?

PITY   Pittance, which is short for everything. But I've always been Pity.

HERSCHEL   Then I have a new shoulder to cry on.

PITY   Thank you for seeing me, Mr. Flechtheim. I've come a long way to find you.

HERSCHEL   An exciting adventure then!

PITY   Yes, it is. I've never travelled alone before.

HERSCHEL   And how are you finding the world, thus far?

PITY   Oh, pretty much as I'd imagined it. Except with people, of course.

HERSCHEL   And how has the European branch of the species been treating you?

PITY   Oh, people here have been great. For the most part, they just ignore me. Except for that woman who let me in.

HERSCHEL   Don't let Vespa scare you. She's our watchdog. Only the truly brave or foolish get past her.

PITY   I think I used up all of my bravery just getting in the door.

HERSCHEL Well, it's a funny thing, isn't Miss Beane. Why is it always assumed that brave people aren't terrified too? The only difference is that brave people have feet that can keep up with their heart.

PITY Or visa versa.

HERSCHEL Exactly. And here you stand, my dear. Feet on the floor, heart through the door. An heroic act indeed!

PITY I'm hardly a hero, Mr. Flechtheim.

HERSCHEL Who knows? The best ones always go unnoticed. Maybe you're just not looking at yourself in the right light.

PITY I'm not here to look at me. Myself, I mean.

HERSCHEL Me, myself and oy! You're an Anglican, aren't you, Miss Beane. So, what brings you here? Your two letters were very mysterious.

PITY I'm sorry about that. It's just that it took me so long to even find you, I had to be sure you were…

HERSCHEL That I was still alive.

PITY Yes, I'm sorry.

HERSCHEL Don't be. I'm alive! Schnapps for everyone!

PITY As I told you, I'm searching for the painting known as Tender. Now, I've been able to track it somewhat during the early-to-mid part of the last century, although there are still great holes in the provenance of this piece.

HERSCHEL Provenance?

PITY I'm sorry. The history of ownership pertaining to a work of art. That's what brings me to Vienna and why I need to see you, because Mr. Flechtheim, the last known owner of the painting is you.

HERSCHEL Fascinating. I'm famous in the art world! Oy, I should buy a beret.

PITY Mr. Flechtheim, please, where's the painting?

HERSCHEL Now, patience Pity. You've just come in from the rain. You're still wet behind the ears. Relax. Take a coffee. You're in Vienna now. It's beautiful here.

HERSCHEL leaves and is placed in his cabinet. LEDA enters from hers, USL.

LEDA Vespa, I heard the bell. Is it him? Did you let him in? What did you tell him? You should have come for me. I wasn't expecting him so soon. Really, it's madness, what sort of person arrives in daylight. Vespa, please keep them away, don't let anyone in. I can't see anyone now. Look at me, I'm not done. Vespa, I hope you haven't… oh, hello.

PITY	Hello.
LEDA	You're… not him.
PITY	I'm sorry.
LEDA	No, please my dear, you mustn't be. The sight of you is a relief. I was worried it was him, and I haven't got the answer yet. And I can't receive anyone, look at me. I'm still in my morning dress. Oh God, mornings are so difficult for me!
PITY	I love the morning. It's the least disappointing time of the day.
LEDA	You must forgive me, my dear. It's so lovely to see you again.
PITY	But we've not met.
LEDA	Exactly, each day is a new beginning, isn't it? Where on earth have you been?
PITY	Um, Canada.
LEDA	I'm so sorry. And how did that go?
PITY	It's not… done. I mean, I've come here, now.
LEDA	And I couldn't be happier! Let me look at you. Darling! How exciting! When are you due?
PITY	What are you talking about?
LEDA	The baby. When shall we expect it?
PITY	I'm not pregnant.
LEDA	No, of course not. You've just let yourself go natural. So many girls do, these days. That's why I didn't recognise you. Well then, let me have a good look. Stay there, don't move! That light, it's perfect for you. You must never leave it.
PITY	I've never been able to stand still.
LEDA	Then you must learn. That's the secret, isn't it?
PITY	Of what?

LEDA	Of everything, dear. Light. Now, granted, this is daylight, never preferred, that. No, artificial evening light is much more easily controlled, nevertheless, you look quite… what is it? Innocent. Very marketable, that. But as I'm sure you already know, when you're not beautiful you must find the other. And for you, in this moment, it's purity in light. You must never leave it.
PITY	Well, I can't just stand in one place.
LEDA	Why not? It's done all the time. Have you ever wondered why beautiful people are always the centre of attention?
PITY	Because they're beautiful.
LEDA	No. Because they always find the best light.
PITY	I don't have those instincts.
LEDA	It's not instinct dear. It's an art. Studied and practiced. Next time you're at a party, look for the most beautiful person in the room. I guarantee they'll be standing in the

	best light, never moving, just letting the rest of the world come to them. I don't know you, do I?
PITY	I'm Pity Beane.
LEDA	What a sad name. Did you live up to it?
PITY	My parents are the sort of people you talk about. Beautifully lit. It was assumed I would be the same.
LEDA	It's a curse to be the plain child of beautiful parents, I know. Better to be deformed or feeble-minded, shockingly ugly or spectacularly wrong in any way. Only two things are noticed in this world. The beautiful and the grotesque. Pity, indeed, the rest of us born plain.
PITY	Who are you?
LEDA	I'm Leda Otenreath. This is my house. What do you want, my plain little girl?
PITY	I've come for the boy.

Scene shift.

Art Slide

A microphone on a small stand is placed on top of the bar. Ronnie speaks for an unseen character.

VOICE And now, Pity Beane, a Master's Degree candidate in the art history, theory and criticism program, will speak on works of missing provenance and institutional responsibility toward original ownership claims. I'm sure this will be quite fascinating. Miss Beane, when you're ready.

Ronnie wears a headrig with PITY'S face in front of it. His hands and the rest of his body are used in conjunction with this face, as if it were a miniature mask. Her voice is amplified during her speech, as if in a lecture hall.

PITY Thank you Professor Turcott. While I am hardly an expert in the field the Professor mentioned in his introduction, my current course of research centres around a specific painting, the provenance of which becomes somewhat dubious after World War II. Further hindering the historical tracking of this painting is a lack of information regarding the artist himself. Steve, may I have the slide now, please.

SFX of slide projector. A rectangle of light frames the painting behind PITY.

Known simply as "Tender," this word being the only marking on the back of the canvas, it may be speculated that this is the title of the piece, or, could indeed be the signature of the artist himself. Personally, I've always believed it to be the latter, although no, I don't have the data to confirm that at present Professor. Research, working, getting there. If, however, the word "tender" represents a title for the canvas, it may be speculated that perhaps the piece is a work unto itself or part of a grouping, not unlike, say, the seven deadly sins or an artistic representation of the virtues, of which, one may conclude, tenderness would be considered most admirable indeed.

We know that the work was painted in 1921, information obtained from records at a London gallery show of new—and therefore unknown—artists. The first owner was Mr. Baltan Fazood, an importer of artifacts from the Middle East. We know that the painting remained in Mr. Fazood's possession until the early 1930s, a mention of it appearing in a 1934 article on his new London townhouse, noteworthy for its stark all-white gallery-like interiors, no doubt a predecessor to the present loft condo craze.

Mr. Fazood was found murdered in that townhouse in 1936, victim of a liaison with with a gay-for-pay piece of trade named Angus MacNamara. At the time of the police investigation, the only "artwork" found were pre-Pollackesque spatters of blood on the previously pristine white walls. Mr. MacNamara was tried and convicted of Fazood's murder, and shortly thereafter,

	and finally true to his profession, I guess you could say he was quite well hung indeed.
VOICE	Miss Beane, please!
PITY	I'm sorry, Professor Turcott. The painting resurfaced in London in 1993 as part of an auction of art and antiquities released from Moscow after the dissolution of the USSR in 1991. The painting was purchased by Mr. Herschel Flechtheim of Chicago, Illinois for £21,000. For the time, this price was considered somewhat of a record given not only the mystery surrounding the artist and the missing provenance from 1934 to 1991, but also because of the subject, composition and somewhat sentimental rendering.

Which naturally has shocked the serious art world, which all too frequently has deemed this painting and other works like it as derivative post-Secessionist decorative illustration, or, as Professor Turcott himself has called it, "Romanticised crap to match the couch salon painting." |
VOICE	Miss Beane, I'm warning you. Tread carefully. No such words may be attributed to me.
PITY	Well, not in print sir. But you did indeed dismiss "Tender" as exactly that when I first proposed this painting as my course of research. Do you not remember chuckling at your own clever re-titling of the piece as "Laddie and the Swan"? Personally, I believe it's the obvious beauty of this painting that is indeed its downfall Sir, because it has no need for an academic to dissect and objectify it like a whore spread-eagled for our pleasure.
VOICE	Miss Beane, sit down please.
PITY	Oh come on Professor! You know, I know, all of us here in this room know, that if any one of us could paint even remotely like that artist, hell, we wouldn't be twitching, bitter academics. No, we would speaking to the world through the end of a paintbrush, not out of our assholes.
VOICE	You will stop now and sit down Miss Beane!

PITY   What is art Professor? To you. Only you. Your personal definition? And don't you dare tell me it's your job, your career, your tenure, your pension. I won't hear that! No, art is the personal contribution to the ever-continuing conversation about life. And I'm having that conversation here today, even if I can't render it on paper or canvas, I want to talk about art, it's my turn. But I will not stand up here and do what all these other monkeys in this department do for your pleasure Professor. I will not stand here and tell you what I think about art. No. I want to talk about how I feel about art, and how it makes me feel. But I'm on thin ice, I know that Professor. Because ever since I've been in this department Sir, my feelings have been a source of ridicule, and dismissed as mawkish and sentimental. And why is that Professor? Are you so afraid of my feelings, are they so dangerous to you? Well you should be afraid Sir, because art is dangerous. And I will tell you here and now, with my colleagues to bear witness, that this painting is dangerously beautiful to me. And why? Because it makes me feel. It makes me feel something I get nowhere else in the world. It makes me feel love. I love this painting. I love that boy!

When all the real people in your world are just so… three dimensional. And they can't help it, but they just keep letting you down. Your dad. Your dead mum. Even Uncle Boyfriend. The fairy fucking godfather who, with all his bitchiness was actually the only one who ever did me any good, but what does he do? He leaves. He left me. And why? Well maybe Professor, because he finally figured out that having all the beautiful things in life that you think and talk about all the time means nothing if all you do is dream of something more. The unspeakable beauty. You know what his note said? The note he left my dad on the kitchen counter? All it said was, "It's just not beautiful anymore." He left me an envelope too. A cheque for $100,000 and a note that said, "Pity, squander this on beauty." That was all he wanted for me, that I would find my unspeakable. But I failed him. I let him down again. And how? What did I do with that money? I used it to come here, because I thought this would be the most sensible road toward art and beauty. But no, all I am met with, day after day, are hearts and minds more blank than a post-modernist canvas.

My God, is growing up in the art world achieved only by embracing the ugly and the unpolished? Is that the road I have to take to be taken seriously? Well, I can't. I won't. Life is already grotesque. Don't tell me to find more ugliness. I don't want to look at ugliness. I don't need to look at it, I already have a fucking mirror, thank you very much. And stop pushing the weird on me. Stop telling me it has to be weird to be art, it has to be weird to be beautiful. I don't need any more weird. And it's not like I don't know weird, I grew up with two gay daddies, for fuck's sake, I know weird shit when it splats on my face, okay?

VOICE   Miss Beane, you will come to my office. Now!

PITY   No professor, the only reason I would ever come to your office again is if you plan on bending me over your desk, lifting my skirt, dropping my panties and fucking me from behind. But that's not what you're going to do, is it Professor? Because I'm just a plain, silly girl, not even attractive enough to dismiss as a beautiful object, and you're just going to kick me out of this department, aren't you? Oh no, it's okay. I think we've both seen this coming Professor, so why don't we just skip that little meeting in your office Sir. You're a very busy man and I'm sure you have lots of things to think and talk about, and it's not like I don't have things to do. I still have a little bit of money left from Uncle Boyfriend and I should just go find my unspeakable. Him.

She points at the painting.

The real thing. That's what I'm going to do. And you know what you can do Professor Turcott? You can go to your office, and you can fuck yourself.

She turns, as if to leave. Simultaneously, the lights shift, placing us back in the present time in the brothel. PITY sees the painting of TENDER.

There you are. Thanks for waiting. I'm sorry it took so long to find you, but beauty, I'm home now.

Ronnie removes the PITY headrig. Shift/transition.

_____ **Lunch Menu**

Music in for the introduction of "The Ladies," the four whores of the brothel, JOHANNA, MUSETTE, IRIS and MAYBELLINE. Each is taken from an US cabinet behind the bar. Ronnie dances them individually to their hanging spots in front of the bar as they are presented to the audience. When all four are in position, and as the music comes to an end, VESPA enters from her SR cabinet.

VESPA Girls, our gentlemen will be arriving soon for lunch, and so, a final inspection, *ja*, before the buffet is laid.

Ah Johanna! How nice to see, Frau Pfefferkuchen, that your slip is clean and that yesterday's *schlagsahne* has been wiped clean from your breast. Ah ah! No arguments, please! Now Johanna, I've decided to lock up the trolley of cakes until after your first appointment. The lawyer will be arriving soon, and he has some briefs that need your immediate attention.

Iris my dear, you, on the other hand, could stand to eat something. I know, you cannot put anything into your mouth and enjoy it. It's the curse of your ballet training. Luckily, I've been able to book you with a British tourist. A few quick pounds and it'll be all be over.

Miss Maybelline, *meine kleine schwartze princessin*! How nice of you to join us. Your presence always adds such elegance to our menu, even if the dish is sold out, *ja*. As usual, Miss Maybelline, your time has been booked exclusively by Mr. Flechtheim once again.

Musette, you are a naughty girl. I've heard you conversing with your customers again. How many times must

I remind you, my pet, it's so impolite to talk with your mouth full. The banker is coming today. He wants to liquidate your assets again.

So ladies, those are the reservations for lunch. This evening's menu, however, is a catastrophe. Not that you're to blame. How could you be to blame? You're beautiful. You're the most beautiful girls in all the world. But tonight, we have had a request for a special feast. Mr. Hiro, a businessman from the East, will arrive soon, and his tongue is not used to the spread we provide. No, this gentleman from the Pacific Rim would like a virgin to serve dinner to him.

PITY is standing US.

VESPA Ah, Fraulein Beane. How can I help you?

PITY Who are these women?

VESPA These are the most beautiful girls in all the world.

PITY They're whores.

VESPA *Ja*, is that a problem for you, Fraulein Beane?

PITY I believe you're the one with the problem, Frau Poopermann. You need a virgin.

VESPA *Ja*, it's true.

PITY Let me do it.

VESPA You? Ha! Why?

PITY I'm a virgin. And you need a virgin, no?

VESPA *Ja…*

PITY So?

VESPA Is it money you're after, Fraulein Beane?

PITY No. Something priceless.

VESPA What?

PITY To be the object of desire, anyone's desire, just once. I want to know what that feels like.

VESPA Why?

PITY Because I can't give it away. So, what do you say, Frau Poopermann? I have something you need, and you have something I want. You let me be one of your most beautiful girls in all the world for one night in my life, and I'll do it for free.

VESPA That's a very interesting offer, Fraulein Beane, but I'm afraid we'll have to discuss that later. With the Madam.

Doorbell SFX.

Ach du leiber! Our gentlemen have arrived. Girls, take your places. Ladies, assume your positions!

Music in, a faster and shorter version of the theme which first introduced the girls. JOHANNA, IRIS, MUSETTE and MAYBELLINE are quickly removed and placed back in the cabinets. VESPA is returned to her cabinet. In exchange, HERSCHEL enters.

HERSCHEL A fascinating house, this, wouldn't you say, Miss Beane?

PITY Mr. Flechtheim, please. It's a brothel.

HERSCHEL No, Miss Beane. This is a refuge.

PITY From what?

HERSCHEL	Child, please. You know, Miss Beane, I've spent most of my time on this earth just waiting for my life to start. Standing still, hoping it would find me. Oh yes, I always thought that one day, life would tap me on the shoulder and say, "Come on Flechtheim, here I am, it's life, let's go, let's be alive at last old man!" But let me assure you, my dear Miss Beane, life will not come knocking on your door. No. Which is why I had to come back here and ring that bell.
PITY	Why?
HERSCHEL	Why? To have lunch.

I met Miss Maybelline in 1937. I was sixteen at the time. Oy, this house was so different then. Schrammel music, cabaret artists, laughter and light, drinking and dancing all through the night. And into all that brightness came the darkest beauty I had ever seen. A dancer from America. Maybelline! Oy, she caused a sensation in this pale, proper town.

We were different as night and day. But even they meet and fold into one at dawn and dusk.

But the following year, my dear Miss Beane, Vienna threw a parade to welcome Herr Hitler. Needless to say, I had to get out of town. I fled to Paris, she was to follow. She never appeared. So I fled further still. To America, her home. And I never saw her again.

PITY	I'm sorry Mr. Flechtheim. Why didn't she follow you?
HERSCHEL	Her movements would have been a little too obvious, my dear, not so easy for her to disappear in the white heat that was Europe in those days. But your painting there, Miss Beane, saved my Maybelline.

You see, the Gestapo had discovered that champagne was on ice in this house, and girls who never considered it gave into vice just to survive. And one of those men, who only knew how to destroy, took a fancy to beauty one night. Your white, gleaming boy. In order for that German officer to be colour-blind, Leda gave him the painting so Maybelline would be spared.

PITY   Mrs. Otenreath owned the house even back then?

HERSCHEL   No, no, no, she had abandoned her married name back in those days. But, she was greatly loved by all those who had not deserted hope. A star in those darkening skies, she was known as Leda Lichter then.

> *Music in, the intro for LEDA's wartime song. All light onstage shifts to a concentrated pool, suggesting a lone spot in a cabaret. A younger version of LEDA turns into the light and sings.*

Until the Sun Returns

LEDA   The sun has closed its eyes
Without the light, the world is grey
And into night we fall
As storm clouds fill the skies
In frosty shrouds, so still we lay
Awaiting springtime's call

Till I thaw on that bright day
You are what my heart must learn
Your arms are warm, so I will stay
Until the sun returns

Hold me through this winter day
For it's you my blue heart yearns
The moon and stars will lead the way
Until the sun returns

> *She is returned to the cabinet from which she came, and time shifts back to present.*

PITY   Oh my God. He came here. After disappearing from Fazood's London townhouse the painting came to Vienna. Okay, I can track that, it's an A to B. There's got to be a trail. But Mr. Flechtheim, what you just said, no way, that doesn't make any sense. Okay, I get the part about Mrs. Otenreath giving the painting to the Nazi guy, but he would have taken it with him. It would have gone somewhere else. But it's here now, and I'm here, and I'm so close but I don't understand any of this.

HERSCHEL My dear, you don't understand the times. That painting was loot, like everything was back then. And after the war, hidden in mountains of art, it was stolen again. Taken off to Russia. Hidden in grey rooms without any light, until the wall came down. That's when I heard about it, so I bought it at auction and brought it home. And when I rang the bell after a lifetime away, Leda was here—Mrs.

                Otenreath again—and so was the dream I had left behind sixty-three years before.

PITY   So, are you going to marry her, Mr. Flechtheim? Make Miss Maybelline an honest woman at last?

HERSCHEL My dear, I was married to an honest woman for fifty-two years. Marry Maybelline? No. I have her hand in mine at last. Till death do us part.

PITY   But Mr. F, don't you have to pay for her company in this place?

HERSCHEL You've obviously never been married, Miss Beane.

PITY   So, do you… you know. Do you and Miss Maybelline have… more than just lunch?

HERSCHEL At my age, lunch is a highlight. But if you're asking if we make love, well, that's none of your business. But I'll tell you this, my inquisitive little Canadian research travelling girl. Miss Beane, please, I'm old, I'm not dead. Of course. All those years, when we were apart, I did have a somewhat special little—how do you say—fantasy.

During the following, HERSCHEL and PITY are hung on the DS chairs. Ronnie uses handpuppets of HERSCHEL and MAYBELLINE to enact the scene.

                I would dream of returning home to Vienna. And she would be waiting for me. And the streets would open up to our joy, as we reclaimed the city as ours. Everything had changed. All the horror and secrets of the past forgotten in the dawn of a new day. Neither she nor I were looked at as different, as less, as disposable. We were simply part of the heartbeat of Vienna, hand in hand.

Music in, and HERSCHEL and MAYBELLINE dance. As the music ends, the handpuppets are removed.

PITY   That's a beautiful story, Mr. Flechtheim. So, did it happen? Did your fantasy come true after all those years?

HERSCHEL Oh Miss Beane. To these eyes, she continues to be the greatest beauty ever seen. Vienna however, while beautiful still, is perhaps unchanged at heart. And so, no, we do not venture out. All we are and all we need is within these walls. This refuge.

He is placed inside his cabinet, as Ronnie continues to speak his voice.

And now, if you'll excuse me, Miss Beane, I do believe I have a luncheon date.

LEDA enters.

LEDA Vespa! Vespa, I've been thinking about our young visitor's offer of assistance. It's madness, she has no experience whatsoever, yet she's willing to hike up her skirts and help however she can. Very Canadian, I suspect. But he wants a virgin to serve him dinner and Vespa, we must be pragmatic, where on earth are we going to find a virgin in Europe at this time of year.

She sees PITY.

Oh, it's you.

PITY You're Leda Lichter.

LEDA I've had many names. That was one. It served its purpose, for a time. But that time is long over.

PITY But it lives on. I've seen your song—"Until The Sun Returns"—performed many times. A very popular drag queen does you.

LEDA So that's the point of living a century then? To be parodied by transvestites.

PITY Oh no, she does it very seriously. It's like total homage.

LEDA It's ridiculous.

PITY You're an icon. The song is timeless.

LEDA The song only meant something because it was specific to its time. And those who heard it, needed it desperately. But it was not unto itself. It was part of a movement. But how could you understand? That's the problem with today. There are no new movements.

PITY That's not true.

LEDA	Really? Look at you, suddenly interested in me because I'm someone worthy of reproduction. Leda Lichter, alive again and appearing nightly in the artless male drag queen's grasp!
PITY	Or alive, without your permission.
LEDA	She was not the most interesting version of me.
PITY	Then why is she the version who is remembered?
LEDA	She was selfish enough to survive.
PITY	She was a hero.

LEDA	She was a runaway, a fraud, a disappointment.
PITY	To who?
LEDA	To herself. Not this old woman, Pity. I don't care what I have become. But the first incarnation, the original version of me as a woman. The wild girl. She would have cared about what I became.
PITY	Why was she wild?
LEDA	Child, the times were wild. I simply listened, and the rhythm of it all changed my heartbeat.

Wild Girl

LEDA	I had been raised a proper British girl, taught to keep myself straight and narrow. For a moment, in my youth, I had escaped the constraints of the cage, but it was a brief lick of liberty. Even after I had been found wandering in the wood, I was returned home and scrubbed clean of the wild. And so I waited for fate's next offer of elopement. Silent, save for pencil, chalk, crayon and brush. Anything to extend my reach and touch what was hidden behind my downcast eyes and frozen smile.
	And so, in those endless days between child and adult, the brush was tamed, my hand steadied and my heart at peace with art. I was becoming a woman, as I learned to speak in a world without ears. I longed to be an artist, for a world without eyes.
	It was my saviour, and at seventeen I painted my dedication. I was gifted, said some. Showed promise, said others. Unoriginal and derivative, said the critics. A blasphemous whore, said my father. When he heard that my painting was to be exhibited in a London show of new painters, I was banished from his home and finally free from his prying hand.

Music in, an early 1920s jazz rhythm, beginning softly and simply, building throughout the following scene.

So I ran again, knowing this time that no one would try to find me. I ran, with money of my own from the sale of that irreligious image. I ran to the temple of all who are wounded yet alive, dead but unable to sleep, penitent to wasted youth and fevered to waste the rest. To find, to feel, to fuck, to forget.

I ran. To Paris.

A marionette of LEDA as a young woman in her late teens appears. Her clothing is of the time, with cloche hat and a straight, unfitted coat, cut just below the knee. This garment will open completely down the front during the scene, exposing her bare breasts and satin knickers. The scene is enacted between Ronnie and the marionette, all set to music.

An awkward, rigid girl in an elegant, curvaceous city. Lady Paris taught me well, for she held my hips, rubbed against me, let me taste her salty sweat and smell her sweetest secrets. And whispered in my ear. "Jazz," she purred, as we began to dance.

And as my posture relaxed and my morals laid to rest, men stood at attention, eager and erect. Their arms flung open, waiting to be crucified by my youth. She watched, my lover Lady Paris, and smiled as these tasty men taught me how to move them. Every night was a heavenly ride to hell and back, and oh, how we danced!

Some were Spaniards, slippery as olives and sharp on the tongue. Some were Germans, all meat and potatoes, deliciously disconsolate. Some were Americans, sweet as pie, proud and loud and up for anything. Most were French. Oh, the French! Bastard baguettes, dipping into whatever they wanted, mouths reeking of smoke and self-importance. It was a smorgasbord of men, and while they thought they were consuming me, I was devouring them.

I never held a brush or stared at bare canvas again. I had painted what needed to be said, and found instead my calling by being not the painter, but the painted. The anointed muse to the drunken tribe of lost boys. I was their model, their inspiration, their comrade, their lover, their mascot, their saint. I became absolution through paint. And oh, how I danced!

I danced with Cubists, who were fading by the time I arrived, but the few who remained were fun. I felt they really saw me, as they looked from all angles, trying to capture every side simultaneously. The finished canvas was usually flat, but on softer sheets, as they flipped and fondled me in search of my whole, they were brilliant to have around.

I danced with Expressionists, who were brutes and loved to torture me. Not in reality, but as a representation of the afflictions they so longed to possess. They worked from their inner state, and when that failed them or proved to be uninteresting, I was splayed on the bed and painted as a mutilated whore, or propped on a crutch, posed as a maimed veteran. They were cynical, socially critical, and sobbed uncontrollably when they came.

I danced with Surrealists, who painted fantastic images from their subconscious minds, none of which made any sense. I understood them completely. They were degenerates, hooligans, layabouts and onanists. The kind of fellows a girl that age should meet. They knew as well as you that you'd never marry them, but chances are they're who you'd close your eyes and dream about once you had found Mr. Right and settled down.

Music ends. Ronnie toasts the audience and drinks.

To art! And the bad boys who make it.

And finally I stopped dancing. Not because the music ended, but because a new song began playing. Some people have a fork in the road to choose from, all I did was pause. Damn our need to breathe, for as I stopped to catch my breath, he caught my eye. He had been staring at me for a long time, I know. But I made the fatal mistake that all doomed lovers commit. I looked back at him. And while I had no intention of following his level path while the mad dancing laughed around me, he froze me with his stare. He was like a song that you don't really like, yet you know all the words and against your will, you sing along.

DOOLEY enters. He's handsome, in the old Arrow Shirt ad kind of way, although a bit too serious and sad. He's dressed in evening wear.

DOOLEY   I am a guest in a ghost town. A town of ghosts, not my own but haunting me without end. Former lovers, not mine, but hers, in numbers almost too many to bear, be it three or three hundred, it matters not, I imagine one set of frozen foreign lips the same as a thousand. I wander her streets filled with named ghosts, and the undead greet me with their smirking glances, their rotting smugness, their sealed, dead youth and their corpse cocks frozen in memory's *rigor mortis*, the ever-present reminder that they were here first. I am alive, surrounded by all the history that touched and kissed and knew her before me. But I am the only one who loves her. I know that, because I dare not reach for her, even though we are the same in this alien grave. She is beautiful, and I am haunted. Oh to die in her arms just once, or forever! Beauty, kill me. One kiss to smother me, please, for I am dead, living in your ghost town and cannot return home until you take my breath away.

LEDA approaches DOOLEY.

LEDA   Why do you stare at me?

DOOLEY   I wasn't aware that I was staring.

LEDA   Liar.

DOOLEY   I'm sorry.

LEDA   Don't be. I like it.

DOOLEY   Why?

LEDA   Because otherwise I would go unnoticed.

DOOLEY	Were you making sure I noticed?
LEDA	No. That's why I can't figure you out. You're different.
DOOLEY	It's quite natural to be drawn toward beauty.
LEDA	Shall I sit for you then? So you may capture my beauty for all time.
DOOLEY	I'm not an artist.
LEDA	Have you tried?
DOOLEY	No.
LEDA	Then how do you know you're not?
DOOLEY	I'm a collector.
LEDA	Of what?
DOOLEY	Of beauty.
LEDA	So you are an expert, Mr....?
DOOLEY	Otenreath. Donald Leopold Otenreath.
LEDA	Swanky. What do your friends call you?
DOOLEY	Dooley.
LEDA	I like that. It makes you less sad.
DOOLEY	If I'm sad, it's simply because I don't know who you are.
LEDA	Leda Swann.
DOOLEY	Very clever.
LEDA	Your appreciation should be directed toward my parents, Mr. and Mrs. Swann. Naming me thus, with their tongues placed firmly in their classical ass-cheeks, was perhaps the only mirthful thing they ever did. Although whimsy certainly was not the intent. I was to be beautiful, as befits the name.
DOOLEY	They are proven then to be prophetic. I shall have to thank them.
LEDA	That will only be possible if you're visiting Hell. They're finally dead.

DOOLEY   I'm sorry.

LEDA   Don't be. At last the ugly duckling has the freedom to fly home, pardoned from her exile of disgrace. Not that I'm in any great hurry. I'm at home here.

DOOLEY   Home is the language in which you think. And you don't think like these people, no matter how hard you try.

LEDA   What do you want from me, Mr. Otenreath?

DOOLEY   What does anyone want from that which they find beautiful? Simply to be recognised.

LEDA   As what, a fellow countryman? Very well, God Save the King! Now on your merry way.

DOOLEY   No, not that.

LEDA   Then what? To be seen as beautiful in return?

DOOLEY   No. As worthy.

LEDA   Of what?

DOOLEY   Of gazing toward the light.

LEDA   You're blind.

DOOLEY   You're right. But what a sight.

LEDA   Shall I be part of your collection Sir, is that what you propose?

DOOLEY   No, a different proposal for you, I think, Miss Swann.

LEDA   Please, I hate that name.

DOOLEY   Then change it.

LEDA   To what?

DOOLEY   Mrs. Otenreath.

LEDA   My word. Can you afford this acquisition, Mr. Otenreath?

DOOLEY   Name your price.

LEDA   Eternal devotion.

DOOLEY   Sold.

Transition. DOOLEY remains, hung in position. LEDA is taken away and hung inside a cabinet. The following is spoken by Ronnie without a marionette.

LEDA Well of course I married him. Who wouldn't? He was handsome enough to cause others to wonder how I would have snared him. Rich enough to afford my bohemian fantasies. Patient enough to suffer my constant reinventions. Smart enough to not delve into my past. Sure enough to believe that I was satisfied with his considerate lovemaking. Sad enough to remain interesting to me. Although my careful devotion to him is no doubt what made him sad. For we were clever, Dooley and I. We did everything right, thinking of one another, when really, all a lover wants is thoughtless desire, not kindness. But I convinced myself that Dooley was the one, because, you see, in certain light, he looked like the one. A manly version of the first boy I kissed. In those moments I loved him, completely, without reason. And then he would move, or be Dooley again. And I would pretend to love him still, because he was good enough to deserve that.

Transition is complete. We are now in the London townhome of DOOLEY and LEDA Otenreath. This is played by Ronnie sans marionette(s), as DOOLEY standing at LEDA's door, her voice as if offstage.

DOOLEY Leda, darling, are you ready?

LEDA In a moment.

DOOLEY Whatever are you doing in there, Mrs. Otenreath?

LEDA A final inspection of the damage in the mirror.

DOOLEY Shall I be your mirror instead?

LEDA Away with you Mr. Otenreath, while I make my final adjustments.

DOOLEY Really darling, it might be more interesting if you allowed me to make a few adjustments of my own.

LEDA Dooley, don't be scandalous, we've a full house this evening. And if their host is not downstairs to ensure that their drinks are filled, you will have a riot on your hands,

	Sir. Darling, you know they can only discuss art through the bottom of a glass.
DOOLEY	I thought they only discussed themselves.
LEDA	Dooley, don't be a bore. They bring some fun into the house.
DOOLEY	Do hurry darling, I'm lost without you.
LEDA	Dooley, don't.
DOOLEY	I don't deserve you Leda. But I vow, I will do anything to stay with you forever.
LEDA	If you stay on the other side of that door forever, I'll never be finished. Trade your melancholy for a martini, darling. I'll be down before the first sip burns the blues from your lips. Now run along, Mr. Otenreath.

DOOLEY exits. Marionette of LEDA walks into the playing area. She is now in her late 20s, although her elegant coiffure and gown suggest an older, more refined woman.

Anton! Darling, you are so sweet to lie. No, I've gained, actually, look at me, I'm a house. No inspection required darling, best keep those hands for the piano. You're playing for us tonight.

Freddie, I knew you'd be here, old thing. Really? Which one? He's a bit old for you, isn't he? He must be enjoying his first pair of long trousers. Yes, yes, I'm sure he's very intelligent Freddie.

Charlie, what are you doing here? We heard you were exiled in France until the play was finished. Oh darling, congratulations. Now we really have cause to celebrate! Help yourself to anything liquid.

Hello, I don't believe we've met. I'm Leda Otenreath. Thank you, we find it cosy. A cunning little cage for the primates at play. Yes, they are an amusing lot aren't they. So madly artistic. Which one of these clever monkeys brought you tonight? Really? I didn't know Dooley had friends of his own.

DOOLEY joins her.

DOOLEY There you are. I was worried we would have to send Ginger up to lure you out of your lair with his gin-soaked sweet talk. He's quite drunk already you know. He's decided to create a mural in the kitchen using whatever he can get his hands on.

LEDA Good. We can sell it for a fortune in the morning.

DOOLEY Ah, I see you've met Mr. Fazood.

LEDA Just. A pleasure. Mr. Fazood is a friend of yours, Dooley.

DOOLEY Our paths cross from time to time. Galleries, auctions, that sort of thing. He has quite an extraordinary eye, haven't you Baltan? Although he's caused me considerable

	grief in bidding at auction Leda, I don't think you should favour him with any more of your attention.
LEDA	You must be a keen lover of things to be such a formidable foe Mr. Fazood. Dooley always gets what he wants, don't you darling?
DOOLEY	Only the things that matter.
	He puts his arm around her.
LEDA	You see, Mr. Fazood? I am one of Mr. Otenreath's trophies.
DOOLEY	No Leda, you are my prize for being alive.
LEDA	So sweet. Regardless, I trust that you will be gentlemen this evening and not engage in battle over me. Why, if blood were to be spilt I'm afraid Ginger might dip in and continue his mural right into the salon.
DOOLEY	You see why I'm mad for her Baltan? Never fear darling, no fisticuffs tonight. For I've already won.
LEDA	Whatever are you talking about, Dooley?
DOOLEY	Our friend Fazood here has possessed a treasure that I have admired for a long time. And due to his kind heart and generous spirit, I am now the owner.
LEDA	I see. So you named a price, Mr. Fazood?
DOOLEY	He was brutal darling. But the cost is immaterial. I wanted it. I have it. Although I shall be sad to part with it.
LEDA	Such mystery Mr. Otenreath! Are you selling it so soon?
DOOLEY	No Leda. I'm returning it to you.
	As though DOOLEY has clapped his hands, he calls the guests to attention.
	My friends, your attention for a moment if you please. As you all know, today is my wife's birthday.
LEDA	Dooley!
DOOLEY	I have been warned under penalty of death not to mention this, and so, before I make my final walk to the hangman's scaffold, I would like to thank her. Thank you Leda. For being the most wonderful woman on earth. For tolerating

me and making me want to be better for you. But most of all, my darling Leda, thank you for looking at me in the first place. And now, because you are my love, and a beauty who loves art, here is something beautiful for you to look at. Again. Happy Birthday Leda!

Immediately after DOOLEY's last line, the painting of TENDER—which has obviously been visible on the stage throughout, but not specifically lit during the previous scene—is suddenly and prominently lit. As they turn upstage, SFX of glass shattering.

Transition. The marionettes of LEDA and DOOLEY are whisked away and hung in a cabinet. PITY enters.

Sensory Recall

PITY I discovered the boy in the painting when I was thirteen. A pivotal age, a seminal time, an instance that has influenced the entire life of Pity Beane. He lived in a book—*Trends in 20th Century Art*—forgotten in the school library, and I was only too happy to have him there. He was safe and untouched by others. The art section of my school library was no-man's-land, small and tucked away, better still for me, so no one could see as I kissed him, day after day after day. And so it was for three years. Secret and perfect and ours.

As I matured and turned sixteen, I felt that I did not know my boy as well as I should. I knew a smell to assign to him, but it was musty and somewhat weak, like the pages of the book in which he lived. If I was going to carry him with me, I would have to find a way to marry all my senses to this angelic boy. So, to liberate him from that tomb-like tome, I decided to create a fragrance and a whisper all his own.

I would pretend to be looking in another direction, intentionally brushing up against boys in the hall, or walking right into their chests. And before they would push me aside, or worse, just ignore me, I would inhale. I would take them into my lungs and know their scent. The jock gods reeking of soap and Dentyne, the slackers oozing of tobacco and booze-stained T-shirts. Asian boys wafting through the halls in a haze of ginger and hair gel, Christian kids, like salt and vinegar chips, brainiacs and geeks who always smelled like fast food litter left in the back seat of a car. And once, by mistake, a teacher. Mr. Van Ryn, tart and familiar like mayonnaise. But the best were the Italian boys in their rayon shirts, smelling sweet and sweaty like sausages hung in the sun to dry. My beautiful boy in the painting could not have smelled like that, but when I morphed them together in my head, I thought I would die.

His voice, of course, was another matter. And although in my fantasy we rarely spoke—we didn't need to, you see, we simply understood everything—still, once in a while he would want to tell me how beautiful I was or how much he loved me. So I needed to hear him. But the problem with modern culture is that every sound has a visual. And I already had the picture. No, hearing my boy was not easy, or perhaps he had nothing to say. And just as I was about to give up, there was a miracle. There was a school play.

My high school had this drama teacher, Mr. Garfinkel, who apparently had studied at a lesser institution of higher learning in a suburb of Toronto and that made him like this total theatre expert. He was always doing collectives and student created work. That's a step up from musicals and murder mysteries I suppose, but, just the same, they were always so lame. But not to Mr. G. In his mind they were totally relevant to our teenage angst.

Anyway, there was a play—or rather, a student collective— called *Beautiful Voices*, a hodge-podge of melting pot stories reflecting the diversity of teenage experience and the one-ness of our global village blah, blah, blah. It was a series of monologues and choral chanting with Yoga-based movement, and featured the usual cast of characters. Amy Tamblidge, this totally annoying bornagain with giant tits talking about her dreams for global peace, as if, Miss fucking Universe! Randall Betrick ranting on about his parents' divorce, again. Trey Fergusson and Amber Witherspoon in this really embarrassing dialogue about teenage suicide without having the courtesy to actually perform it for us. Oh, and get this, Blaine Harker confessing that he was gay—oh puh-leese, like that was news—and now we were all supposed to like him even though he was just as annoying as before but out, and on and on and on. But near the end, there he was. My miracle. A boy who had never dipped his toe into the cesspool of drama club before, but had been coerced into the group by Mr. Garfinkel because of his brooding intensity and sullen mystique. Which meant he was totally hot, in that damaged and dangerous kind of way.

The boy's name was Angelo Bajrektarevic. He was the son of Yugoslavian immigrants, and although he had been in school as long as I could remember, no one seemed to know him. I stood next to him once on the football field during a weekly bomb threat, and he smelled divine. Like cheese. Not wholesome and annoying like cheddar, or stinky like Stilton, no, kind of foreign and funky, like Camembert wrapped in cashmere. I'll admit I had a minor crush on him, but I already had a boyfriend. The angel in the painting. And like Uncle Boyfriend always said, fantasising about someone real only leads to disappointment.

I have no idea why I went to see *Beautiful Voices*, but I'm really glad I did. Because somewhere near the end, after all the whining drama club assholes had tortured us, Angelo Bajrektarevic came out into a pool of light, set his gaze beyond the audience and then he did it. He spoke. He spoke of loss, of grief, of the sadness that he would never know the homeland his parents had fled. And why? For what? Invisible lines, that's why people bled. Erecting borders between brothers where none had been before. Drawing lines in the sand, that's what men call war. And then he levelled his gaze with ours—no, not ours, with mine, I swear—and he simply, softly, surely said "This school is full of stupid assholes. Nothing is beautiful, but you only know that when you're dead." And then he took a gun out of his jacket and pointed it at us. No, not us, he pointed it at me. Like he was going to shoot me through the heart with his truth. I don't know if that was the end of the play or not, because everyone started screaming and rushing for the exits. But I just sat there, frozen.

Fuck that was a good play.

Rumour had it that Mr. Garfinkel actually shit himself backstage. Angelo, of course, was expelled, and he never came back to school. I think about him though. He's going to have a hard life, because he figured things out far too soon and that's no way to get along. But I wish I could have told him that part of what he said that night was wrong. There is beauty in the world. You just have to know how to make it up. Like, whenever I close my eyes and dream of my angelic painted youth whispering in my ear, it's always and forever Angelo's voice I hear.

PITY leaves. Transition. Interior of a train, moving. On top of the bar, LEDA (as a table-top figure) sits alone.

Wicked Winter

LEDA Wicked winter
Despised and scorned
Find me now and find within
A warm reception to your
Simple chill

You cannot take my heart
For others have tried
And all have failed
It beats, but only to mock life
Not sustain it

So, like a lover
Place your cool lips on mine

Let me inhale you
Feed me with your frost
And freeze me
My useless heart and empty breath
Already a wasteland
Waiting, for you

Wicked winter
Despised and scorned
I will not love you, I promise that
But give instead this gift
Of frosty respect

Cattle Car

Ronnie puts on the headrig of AUNTIE SARI, the cow.

SARI   I loathe travelling by train. Too much time for reflection in the glass, watching the world pass you by.

LEDA   Auntie Sari. What are you doing here?

SARI   I was about to ask you the same thing, my dear. This is a rather common means of transportation Leda. Surely you might have arranged a private car. You're married to a very substantial man.

LEDA   I shall have to employ thrift for awhile, Auntie Sari. Besides, I've had quite enough luxury. Travelling first class can be costly to a woman.

SARI   You are quite the most ridiculous girl. I don't know why I bother with you.

LEDA   Then why do you?

SARI   Because you can see me. And hear me. You rarely listen, mind. I don't know why I waste my breath.

LEDA   Perhaps because I give it to you.

SARI   And, as such, I feel a duty to use it in your interest.

LEDA	My conscience is a cow.
SARI	You could do worse, my girl.
LEDA	I have, Auntie Sari.
SARI	Then let's just enjoy the ride. Leda. Leda, where are we off to?
LEDA	Vienna, I think.
SARI	Vienna? Not Paris?
LEDA	I'm known in Paris.
SARI	Precisely, we could have some fun.
LEDA	I want to be unknown. Besides, I thought you loathed Paris, Auntie Sari.
SARI	I do! But Paris is a place you can love and hate at the same time. Like a real lover. That's the beauty of it. But Vienna? Oh Leda, it's all waltzes and cake and memories of a lost empire. There's nothing to do!
LEDA	Vienna is a beautiful old dowager, exiled from reality. She'll teach me to fade gracefully as we crumble to dust.
SARI	And what does Dooley think of this madness?
LEDA	I don't know, I didn't tell him. I left without saying goodbye.
SARI	Leda! Scandalous girl! Why must you visit another outrage upon our family name?
LEDA	It won't be on your name, Auntie Sari. Nor Dooley's. I've taken Mother's maiden name. Lichter. Father couldn't bear it of course, it sounded so Germanic. But dear Mother has finally done me a favour. Leda Lichter. I'll fit right in.
SARI	I thought you wanted anonymity.
LEDA	You are only left alone if you appear to belong in the first place.
SARI	And are you alone now?
LEDA	Apparently not, Auntie Sari.

SARI   You know what I mean. Don't play games with me, my girl.

LEDA   But Auntie Sari, you are a game. My childhood imagining. That's why you exist.

SARI   And you imagine me a cow. Such cheek!

LEDA   Why complain? I dress you well.

SARI   Yes, you've always had style, I give you that.

LEDA   It's all a plain girl can aspire to. The stylish, elegant hostess.

SARI   Then why such an inelegant move as this?

LEDA looks out of the window.

LEDA   Dooley loves me Auntie Sari. The version I gave him. The object of his affection. I want him to remember her.

SARI   Ah, so that's it.

LEDA   What?

SARI   The point of this folly. Running from age.

LEDA   No. From youth.

SARI   Then why have you brought it with you?

LEDA   You sat next to me Auntie Sari. I didn't invite you.

SARI   I'm not referring to me. It's that painting, isn't it? Youth. You've brought it with you.

LEDA   I cannot escape him.

SARI   A maiden aunt must learn to chew her cud at times. But Leda, mark my words, that painting has never brought you happiness.

LEDA   I am happiest on my own, Auntie Sari.

SARI   Wicked gibberish! You delight in shocking me, don't you? Leda, you can't be alone. You're a woman! You need someone to take care of you. Which is why I've brought the monkey.

LEDA   What are you talking about you silly old cow?

Ronnie places a handpuppet of PLATO on his hand.

SARI — What are you, deaf, blind, dumb? This monkey! I'm gifting you with a little monkey to accompany you on this mad adventure.

LEDA — I can't take care of a monkey.

SARI — Of course not. He'll take care of you. He's very clever, as monkeys go. He sings you know.

LEDA — Monkeys can't sing.

SARI — And maiden aunts shouldn't be cows. But that's your gift, Leda. You can hear us. And my gift to you is this little singing monkey. Sometimes it's nice to hear a song from the past. Just to remind you of where you've been, my little woman of mystery. Well, time for tea. I hope they have scones. They go so nicely with my clotted cream.

LEDA — What's his name? The monkey.

SARI — You're the one who's so very clever with names. Leda Swann. Leda Otenreath. Now Leda Lichter. Haven't you one to spare?

LEDA — Come on, old thing. I know you've thought this through. Otherwise you wouldn't be giving him to me.

SARI — Call him Plato. Perhaps with time, he'll help you find the reality of your ideals.

LEDA — Thank you Auntie Sari.

SARI — You're welcome my dear.

SARI kisses her.

Safe passage to you Leda.

SARI leaves. PLATO sings to LEDA.

Say Goodbye

PLATO Let me go, if you leave
Say goodbye, then be gone
Do not stand in the wings, do not linger on
Let the fire's final hiss
Die away, like your kiss
Say goodbye when you leave
Then be gone

LEDA You're a funny little thing, aren't you? Like a man in a monkey suit. So, this is my destiny then. To travel in the company of a beauty and a beast.

> *LEDA and PLATO are put away. Transition. PITY approaches the elderly LEDA, singing the last lines of the song.*

Animal Crackers

PITY Say goodbye when you leave, then be gone.

LEDA Plato, how lovely.

> *She turns and sees PITY beside her.*

Oh, hello dear.

PITY I like your monkey. He sings beautifully, I think.

LEDA You can hear him?

PITY Well sure. Can't you?

LEDA Yes. But I thought I was the only one. Have you always heard the animals sing?

PITY No, I was taught.

LEDA How?

PITY Uncle Boyfriend. He was like you, in a way. At some point he just decided that animals were better. Easier.

LEDA Angels.

PITY	Yes. I suppose. And he could hear them. Not converse really, not communicate, but hear. And he taught me.
LEDA	To speak.
PITY	To follow the voices. I was seven when it began. We started with dogs of course, because they're easiest to understand. And generally the nicest, on the whole. I love listening to dogs, don't you? And, over time, I became fluent in mice, birds, even some large zoo animals.

LEDA	Elephants are so droll, *n'est-ce pas?*
PITY	And hippos, oh my God, bitter as hell but fucking hilarious!
LEDA	Did you master cat?
PITY	Not really. Cats are difficult. Except when they're in trouble. Then they're totally understandable.
LEDA	What else do you hear?
PITY	Thoughts, warnings, crying, the usual.
LEDA	Crying? Whose?
PITY	Animals, mostly. And sometimes, boys. Whole choirs of them, crying.
LEDA	Dying.
PITY	Yes.
LEDA	I've never heard that.
PITY	You're lucky. It's not as romantic as it sounds. But it's been increasing lately. I hear crying choirs of boys more often than animals. Sometimes you just want to sit and have a pigeon whisper to you or listen to a rabbit giggling.
LEDA	You'll be mad one day. You know that.
PITY	I hope so. Personally though, I don't know if I would have dressed him up. The chimpanzee. Plato. I don't know if I would have put him in that suit. It seems a bit humiliating, dressing him up like a devolved little man.
LEDA	He came to me that way. Who am I to monkey with evolution?
PITY	That cow is a piece of work. Has she been around long?
LEDA	Oh God, don't tell me you can see and hear Auntie Sari too?
PITY	She's kind of hard to miss.
LEDA	You can see my memories?
PITY	Your memories are totally cool. It's like watching sad old black and white movies on TV with Uncle Boyfriend.

LEDA	But you barely know me.
PITY	Well lady, I know you talk to a cow.
LEDA	I made her up. When I was a little girl. She helped me through some very unpleasant times. Plato was a gift from Auntie Sari.
PITY	Whoa. Your imaginary cow gave you a real monkey? Fuck, that's good.
LEDA	Oh stop, it's nothing, really.
PITY	Shut up, you're fabulous! I mean, Uncle Boyfriend was pretty good, but even he couldn't make his imaginary world interact with physical reality.
LEDA	Now Pity, if you can hear the animals talk and see my memories, I suspect you've already dabbled in forging fact with fancy.
PITY	A bit.
LEDA	I knew it!
PITY	Don't get too excited, it was a complete disaster. I created a lifeless shape and then tried to give it breath.
LEDA	Rarely successful, that. Breathing life into static icons. Only the Pope or select puppeteers can do it, but even at best it's still just sleight of hand. Better to begin with one's reality and layer on top. I was a pink puppy for awhile. And how? My hair. Strawberry blonde, you see.
PITY	I was a beaver.

Beaver Tales

PITY	Queen Elizabeth High School had a football team. The Queen Elizabeth Beavers. The obvious cheap comedy of the name was seemingly lost on school officials. I, however, had the distinct cultural advantage of being raised on show tunes, Carry On movies and classic

animation, so my sense of humour was as camp as a boy scout tent.

I've never had much team spirit, because frankly, no team ever wanted me. But it seemed a glaring omission to my refined aesthetic that the football team didn't have a mascot. Queen Elizabeth had no beaver, and I made it my personal mission to rectify the situation.

In his heyday, Uncle Boyfriend was a bit of a Miss Thing when it came to clothes, and luckily for me, the entire history of men's fashion excesses for the last thirty years was stored in our basement. From that stash, I chose a long, loose-fitting grey Italian wool overcoat, circa 1984, with shoulder pads the size of a small Cessna's wingspan.

Mr. Kelecki at the Budget Upholstery Barn gave me a garbage bag full of foam rubber scraps, and with assistance from the *Muppets Make Puppets* book and a hot glue gun, I fashioned a reasonable facsimile of a modern character mascot. Okay, it wasn't exactly Disney on Ice quality, but if you squint you can detect the obvious parallels to contemporary Czech stop motion animation. And courtesy of a brief flirtation with Goth culture in the eighth grade, I had a floor length black crushed velvet cape at the back of my closet, perfect for reincarnation as a tail. And thus, Queen Elizabeth's beaver was born.

> *PITY appears in a beaver costume. It is threadbare, obviously homemade and somewhat nasty. The cartoon proportions hint at cuteness, although the rather demented beaver head held under her arm, with maniacal teeth and eyes, creates a creepy picture. The quilted velvet tail trails behind her.*

I think a lot of people actually liked having a mascot, although admitting that wouldn't have been cool. So, at every opportunity, someone would push me over. I quickly learned that mascot work affords limited peripheral vision, so there's never a hope in hell of sensing an attack. Luckily the peanut shaped foam underbody of the costume padded my fall. But I would just pick myself up, clench my two front teeth—metaphorically speaking, of course—and soldier on.

The combination of foam rubber, wool and perspiration very quickly resulted in a really ripe rodent. And it didn't take long before I began to hear the snickering in the halls or as I entered class, "Hey, isn't that the chick with the smelly beaver?" followed by the chortle and snort punctuation so adored by underachievers and athletes. But it didn't make me want to stop, in fact, it was even more reason to put on my stupid costume and become something other than myself. Besides, I had already clued into the ugly truth that I was never going to be beautiful, but at least in this suit, I had the potential for cute.

We had a game against the Wailers from Our Lady of Perpetual Sorrow, a Catholic high school across town. I wasn't invited exactly, but I schlepped my beaver in three big garbage bags on the number 57 bus. I got to the school before any of the team, and a custodian told me I could suit up in one of the locker rooms. I'd finally clued into the heat factor, and decided to wear the costume with nothing on underneath. So, there I was, naked in my beaver suit, all alone in a strange locker room. I put the head on, checked myself in the mirror, and sat down on the floor. And apparently fell fast asleep.

When I woke up, I knew I wasn't alone. The team had arrived and were going at it in full teenage boy throttle. Swearing, goofing around, snapping towels, the usual. But even with my limited visibility through the mesh strainer eyes, I could see them. Undressing, partially clothed, naked. C'mon, it's not like I hadn't seen a guy naked before. I mean, the boy in the painting was naked, but, okay, yes, this was the first time I'd actually seen a real guy without clothes. And there was something so, I dunno, sweet about they way their bums danced under the skin, how their boy chests spread like butter on a hot knife when they moved their arms, and the wholly new view of those penises just, well, hanging there. They weren't as big as I had been told they were, but they were cute. I had a hunch that penises and I were going to get along just fine. I wanted to tell Uncle Boyfriend about this, but I knew I never would. How could I? How could I admit that all these boys saw was a big lumpy foam rubber costume just lying in the corner. How could they know that I was already inside, that I had very slowly and almost automatically drawn my right hand up inside the sleeve and down into the round cavern of the body. How could anyone know that I was rubbing myself inside that beaver suit. How could anyone know, when I wasn't even aware of it myself?

This was the moment. Mum, can you see? My unwitnessed passage from child into woman. And just as I was about to come to that beautiful new threshold, I heard someone say, "I dare you to kick that fucking beaver," followed by "No fucking way, that thing stinks. Besides, I hear it has

AIDS." Peels of laughter rang out. "No shit man, I heard that chick has two fags instead of real parents." Hoots and howls all around, "Yeah, my Dad said they're total cocksuckers man. I bet that girl isn't even a real girl. She's probably like a fag too. I mean, come on, she's too fucking ugly to be a chick man." And, like a scene from Lord of the Flies, crazy chanting "Kill the fag! Kill the fag!" began. I didn't have time to be afraid, I was still verging on my impending first moment of bliss when they started kicking. Kicking me, kicking what they thought was an empty costume lying on the floor. Naked wild boys, tight skin stretching like rubber bands, snapping into me. Mr. Kelecki's foam rubber couldn't cushion that much hate. I felt every blow, and clenched my teeth so as not to cry out. "Kill the fag! Kill the fag! Kill the fag!" until heat and pain shocked me unconscious.

In my fantasy of this story since, I awaken finally, bloodied but brave, and find my way to the playing field, game already underway. And my paint stick teeth become knives, my foam rubber claws are real and deadly, and I take my revenge on boys and cheerleaders. Their shoulder pads and pompoms are no match for the natural armour given to me by nature, and they die. They die horribly, knowing in their final moments that behind the mesh strainer eyes is the girl, now made woman by all this blood.

Actually, the custodian discovered me during the game. He heard some whimpering from the beaver suit on the floor and found me inside, naked and bleeding. My crossing over into womanhood did not occur by orgasm, but with three broken ribs, a dislocated shoulder, two broken fingers and severe trauma to the head, back and hips. I was in hospital for three weeks, in bed at home for a long time after that, and finished high school by correspondence courses and tutors. No charges were ever laid. The team had made it to Playoffs. And that was all that mattered.

PITY beaver is placed in a cabinet. Another version of PITY is taken from the same cabinet. She is now dressed—awkwardly—like one of the whores. LEDA, still CS, speaks.

LEDA Where did you find that ridiculous costume?

PITY Up there. In that room.

LEDA My room. No one in this house is allowed in there.

PITY But I'm working for the house tonight, and I wanted to find something so I would be beautiful for Mr. Hiro.

LEDA You miss the point of his request, my dear. He does not want a painted whore. He desires your naked innocence.

PITY But how shall I greet him?

LEDA You will not greet him. Stay silent. You must be an object beyond his grasp. He will pay simply for the pleasure of knowing that.

PITY But I thought he wanted a virgin to deflower.

LEDA No, Pity. He will not touch you. Keep your eyes closed, do not look at him. If he finds you beautiful, it is to remind himself of how unworthy he is. Beauty never looks back at us, we stare at it and hope. Surely you know how that feels.

PITY Can I at least wear the stockings?

LEDA Oh God. How did you find those?

PITY I didn't mean to snoop, honest. But I couldn't resist. They're like the ones he's wearing in the painting.

LEDA Those are the ones he wore.

PITY You knew him?

LEDA I was there.

PITY Where?

LEDA Inside that scene. Against that tree.

PITY I can't see that memory.

LEDA It's not a memory, you stupid girl! He's alive! He's my breath.

PITY	Who is he?
LEDA	He is Tender.
PITY	Artist and subject were the same?
LEDA	No. I signed his name to my witness of him.
PITY	You're the artist.
LEDA	I am an old whore. My brush became silent a long time ago. I painted him, then no more.
PITY	Why?
LEDA	So he could continue to speak.

> *LEDA and PITY are left DS in front of the bar. Ronnie goes behind the bar and reveals a doll figure of child LEDA. The whole scene (undressing, travel by boat across the channel, etc.) is played on top of the bar with this single jointed figure. The voice is LEDA's, in present time.*

I stopped being a girl in 1917. The world was at war and I was thirteen. Marie was my nanny, she called me her puppy. Her little pink puppy with strawberry hair. And that was enough at that age in between. Neither child nor adult, I would lay in my bed and wonder what being a woman would mean. In the shadows above, I imagined my husband or lover or both. They looked like my father and smelled just the same. That was my game at night and those were my dreams, when I was thirteen.

Wide awake, I would see him, but my eyes forbade me to look. Quiet now, in the dark, I would stroke my own hair, reach down into my nightgown to feel breasts that were not there. I could not wait for them to grow, but I was just a girl. Daddy's little girl. And these were not my hands.

My nanny Marie in the doorway, watching me feel where breasts should be. But I was not moving as the room sprang to life. No words, only breath, gulping and short above me, a gasp at the door. Hands disappeared, the breathing stopped and my feet hit the floor.

Marie stole me from my bed, without a word, nothing said. Just a look, hurry now, this is not a game. Plucked from the china cabinet world of childhood, never to be prized porcelain again. Trousers on my legs, scissors hurriedly hacking at my curls, concealed in a truer version of myself than when I was a girl. My hair was cut short, and childhood left behind in a puddle of tendrils and frills on the doll house floor. All was left behind as we ran. The little pink puppy looked like a boy and ran like a man.

I never asked why. She never explained. We knew, woman and girl, that men are horrible, be they at large or at home. And so we ran, into the warring world, together. Alone.

Passage by night across the channel, illegal and daring and foolish and heart-in-your-throat exciting. I do not know what lies or truths Marie had told to gain our place upon that merchant vessel. What did she pay for our passage that night? No woman's freedom is without a price. No hand extended unless a coin or a breast is placed in it, no knight in armour appears until a damsel lies, he does not take a shining unless there is a prize. I slept in her cloak and did not see the journey, shrouded from sight I did not witness the fare being paid as England grew dim in the darkness and to France we were conveyed. There were no stars, only salt air in the black.

We did not walk on water. We ran, and never looked back.

On land at last again, our feet never stopped. My first taste that running does not make one free. Simply fugitive from the inevitable sentence. We ran like open prey all day until, at last, we were surrounded by trees. I did not know which wood it was, nor did I know what would become of us there, only that no fate could be so great as that which lay in wait in Britain. Of that I was certain. The indecorous hand of the incubus. My Father. No passage by wartime sea nor flight through unknown scarred terrain could be as frightening as he, who stood over my bed and breathed. Shallow, short, spurting over me. No tree in unknown wood could threaten more than this. And so we ran. My hair, cut short, shorn of all female propriety. I looked like a wild boy. And was hungry like a man.

But sounds of other hungry men thundered through this place. For war was near and we could hear the guns and cannons scream. Come with me, said Marie, but as night's fingers covered the wood, I lost grip of my nanny's hand. Marie, Marie, where are you? Don't leave me, Marie! Your little pink puppy is lost, alone in this strange land.

There was no sight to see, just sounds and smells. No light. No Marie. Just me and fallen leaves. I dare not move in darkness, for every crunching step revealed my place. My feet had touched the water, not the sea nor river, but something wet and still. I drank and fed my thirst from the awful, fetid swill. And so I sat and waited, in the bed of leaves I'd made. All the distant thunder dead, I held my breath and prayed. Not to God, oh no, not him, but to my father instead. Oh Father, please let me come home. Where I can be warm and you can touch me in my bed. My hair will grow back, Daddy I promise, I'll keep myself for you. My little hands, my secret mouth, my not yet woman's breasts. Just come and find me Father, and do what you must do. And as I prayed this terrible hymn to the horrible he who hurt me, that he would not desert me, as I had done to him, sleep came at last and on this leafy bed I laid my head to rest.

> *The doll of LEDA is curled into a sleeping position. A doll of TENDER, dressed in his Highland Battalion uniform, is revealed and acted on top of the bar.*

TENDER Little toy soldiers, all in a row. Perfect pewter playthings pushed to the front, mapped on a board like a game. Some to fall, some to advance, to retreat is defeat, so push into France. Little toy soldiers, all in a row. To battle, to battle we go.

A little toy soldier dressed for the game, to run and jump and crawl in unknown fields of death. But I am young and full of breath, and so my country sent me, like a perfectly wrapped bequest. Wed to this war in my tartan trousseau. To battle, to battle I go.

A little toy soldier dressed like a man. Don't think of me as real, that would cause you to care. What then if I fall, to die in the mud, another land's hands stained with my blood. No, don't think of such things, make me a toy. A poster, a stamp, a song filled with joy. Speak of your flag or your country or king, speak of every ridiculous thing but the truth. Sit on your hands and make war while your youth die. Keep me a lie. Don't sing of me, for then I am real. Don't say my name, don't think, don't feel. I'm just a toy, and when broke I'll be gone. That's the beauty of war. We only remember the posters, the stamps, the songs filled with joy. I'm your little soldier toy dressed like a man. How can you mourn a boy you don't know? To battle, to battle I go.

If you must play at remembrance day, let go of your God and let the devil win. For there is no sense in war. The smell of burning flesh and hair, like sour toast, bonfires of boys left to roast. Keep your homefires burning if you can, the kindling has been sent to other lands. You must never hear the screaming or the moans. The gurgling of your son shot in the throat. Clutch that last letter he wrote, make him a song, he won't sing anymore. No mother, sing, for you sent him to war. And whatever his last words might have been, forever you never will know. For your honour madam, to battle, to battle we go.

It was beautiful. It was silence and stillness, and I thought I was home. I dreamed of the prairie, wished for that sky, people who knew me, but I was not there, I was here on my own. I lifted my head, wanting angels above, but they only lay dying around. This moment had found me alone in the trench, bodies of comrades still, by my side.

Cushioned on impact by boys like myself. A little toy soldier alone on the shelf, the others all toppled and red. Warm from the last moment of life, from urine and feces and chests opened wide. An army of toys all dead. Wild-eyed boys, staring at me, begging for one last look. There was no singing then, I didn't hear a thing. Didn't hear the second blast as poison shell was lobbed my way. Only saw the air become death as the cloud hovered and fell. Forget the smell. Ignore the sounds, the constant ringing. This devil had yellow fingers. Die. Die. Dichlorethylsulphide. Mustard gas, the blistering touch, reaching out and dragging me down below. "Take my hand," the devil said, "and to Hades, to Hades we'll go."

No.

Does a boy decide to be a man? Or does nature simply take his hand and guide him? Can a man decide to be afraid? Or is the softer heart's destiny made when simply pushed in the opposite direction that heroes choose. There were no shoes for me to fill, no footsteps clearly marked. I simply ran, in the twilight yawning somewhere between boy and man. Shell-shocked out of all senses, I ran, I ran, I ran, until I could run no more. I ran. Until the devil's fingers could not reach me.

Mum!

At last my gulping breath was calm and night pushed closed my eyes, When I awoke I saw the dawn, the ringing in my ears was gone, and morning's mist was all around. There was no sound, but this. The crunch of fallen leaves under footsteps coming near. Not an army like before, nor the sound of distant war, just one man walking toward me as I lay there on the forest's floor. "Are you hurt?" he asked, and I said no, simply taking rest. "I will not be addressed that way, stand up, salute, explain yourself, what have you to say?" I stumbled to my feet to find a man whose age and rank were greater than my own. Not a boy, nor soldier toy, he was an officer from the army of men, different, better, higher, yes, but also from my home. He was me, he was mine, familiar and living and true, but when I reached out for his hand he struck me down again. "Look at you!"

he spit, his foot was on my chest. "A coward running through the woods, a runaway, no less. You will not defile those clothes anymore, will not ridicule these garments of war. Stand up, strip down, undress!" I tried to speak again, to tell the hell I saw, but when I moved my mouth his fist was swift and hit my jaw. I bled at last in war, beaten by my own. "Coward, coward, coward" he crowed, as my uniform hit the ground. Blood and leaves and tartan swirled all around. I was not his brother, his comrade or his friend.

A naked boy in foreign wood, cloaked in shame and autumn air. Not a man, nor a toy, neither soldier, just a boy. Shivering, hairless, pale and lost, waiting for this jury of one to speak the price, extract the cost for running from death to this. From his rucksack the man took something soft, something green, and threw it in my face. It smelled of something beautiful, the city, a woman, powder, life lived far from this strange place. "If you can't be a man" he said, "then you must be a girl. Hairless and pale and afraid. But you're less than a girl, so put on these stockings and then you'll be made like the whore I took them from in Paris." And for a moment, he smiled and was delicate as I fumbled with the silk, embarrassed by his game. I was not a toy soldier, but a doll yet again. He knelt between my legs and smoothed the green shroud as it enveloped my skin, touching only stocking, never flesh, no part of me on him. And slowly standing, turned me round and bent me toward a tree. The bark was rough against my cheek, but not so coarse as his trouser's wool, scratching at my back, rubbing against me.

And then, I bled again. Ripped wide by what, I did not know. Oh no, oh no, not that, not him in me. His hands on my hips, pounding from the rear. I screamed, but no one heard, only trees were near. "Coward, coward, worse than a girl" he whispered as he took me at the tree. This was not love, this was not sweet, a little toy soldier's final defeat. This was not beautiful, I am not your Christ. No God cried for me as this son paid the price. No poppy grows to resurrect me, as my countryman fucked me and finished my youth. Who was the coward now, there is your truth. Brave soldier he was, and honoured back home, butchered a boy, buggered his own. Sing him a song, he knows all the words. And a secret verse you never have heard. "Coward, coward, worse than a girl," everyone sing along.

The melody of me will not linger on. You will not remember my name.

Arms overhead, left for dead, forgotten little soldier boy, tied up to the tree. Cast-off broken soldier's whore, toyed

	with in the leaves. A carpet of red and gold underneath my feet, branches blazing with their dead ready for release. But I cannot return to dirt and rot into the ground, for I am held against the bark, no earthly grave to mark the spot where the little toy soldier fell down.
	TENDER stays tied against Ronnie's chest as the doll of sleeping LEDA awakens.
LEDA	And then, I awoke, frozen from the night before. My skin so white, my fingers blue, transparent in the light. I have never thawed since that day when I woke up alone and lost. All the past behind me and across the pond a vision sent to show the way. Through the mist an angel, dying by a tree. A final sign to prove that God was dead inside of me. I stood and walked on liquid ground, the water froze and all around the air was filled with snow. Neither wild boy nor girl, nature's hand escorted me to the other side. I was woman as I walked on water toward the wingless angel guide.
TENDER	Lace patterned flakes danced around head. But if to hell I go and I am dead, there were no flames as fires hissed, but from the snowy waters' mist rose a creature soft and white. My God had not forgotten me, but came down as a swan. Let life's last touch not be the hand that took my will to live, but your sweet kiss to forgive and lift me toward the light.
LEDA	He bade that I should kiss him before his life was gone. "I am Leda" said my nearing lips, but he said "No, you are the swan." This angel boy had skin so thin I felt I could see inside of him. Surely he was beauty, surely he was love, surely he was good. What had he done to heaven to be cast out, left bleeding in the wood. If heaven's mercy could not hear an angel's final plea, I understood, from that day, it never would find me.
TENDER	This swan was my lone Valkyrie, standing in the wait. And trees and leaves and snow and she were witness to my fate.
LEDA	Drawing close to him I touched the skin of the angel nearing death. And as my lips received his kiss, he shared his final breath.

TENDER I am Tender.

LEDA He said, and then there was no more. His closing breath became my first, at last I was as woman cursed as my body cramped and bled. Pray Valhalla greet him, as to final battle, like chattel, he'll go. Angel dead and dying swan, bleeding in the snow.

> *Ronnie blows a handful of small white feathers above the scene, and they float onto and around TENDER and young LEDA. The jointed figures are removed and Ronnie returns to LEDA and PITY in front of the bar.*

PITY You're wrong, you know.

LEDA	How so?
PITY	You said beauty never looks at us. But he looked into you.
LEDA	And saw a swan, not me.

SFX of the doorbell.

It appears that Mr. Hiro has arrived. Pity, you don't have to do this.

PITY	Let him in, Mrs. Otenreath. Let him look. Make him pay. He won't touch me.
LEDA	Pity, wash your face. Don't drown yourself in paint.

LEDA and PITY are placed in cabinets. Doorbell SFX.

Ronnie presents a tray and places it on the bar. We see a nude doll figure of PITY, flat on her back. Taking a small serving dish, he places a small piece of food on her body. The tray is rotated so that her head is DS on the bar. Turning US, Ronnie puts on the headrig of Mr. Hiro. He turns and bows toward PITY, then, placing his hands on the bar, leans down to smell her. His hand above her face, as if caressing but without touching, it travels down the length of her body, his breath audible throughout. He takes the piece of food and slowly raises it to his mouth. Ronnie thrusts his head back and puts it into his own mouth. Hiro puts his hands together, bows, and takes out a money bill and throws it onto PITY. He bows, turns and leaves.

Removing the headrig, Ronnie turns back toward the bar. PITY sits up, and as she is lifted by Ronnie, faces the painting of TENDER US.

PITY	Now I know how it feels.

She turns toward the bar.

Poor you.

The doll and tray are removed.

Ronnie puts on a headrig of (old) LEDA. It has a "dress" of flowing chiffon hanging from it. His hands become hers.

Holes

LEDA There are holes in my shoes
That's provenance, dears
Age-hardened leather grows thin through the years
For too many dances
Blister the soul
And covering your tracks in the dirt takes its toll
How droll, I admit
Counterfeit, a fraud on the stroll
I've traded the past, squandered my history
Always well-heeled but shrouded in mystery
With no one to know, no one will miss me
Oh dear
No, running's my best-suited role

There are holes in my heart
This provenance, alone
A beating, bloodless fist chewed to the bone
Bludgeoned but not beaten
Buried alive
Pounding bloody marvel willed to survive
Revive, it dares me
It wears me and will not be deprived
My heart isn't true, but one truth I've known
Red goes with everything, blue's best alone
Heart on wing, the ugly cygnet has flown
So alone
No, this is my secret swan dive

There are holes in the story
This provenance, mine
Gaps in the journey forgotten with time
Beginnings unfinished
Endings not met
Bushels of middles I choose to forget
And yet, I cannot
I forgot to bury regret
I've dampened my laughter, dried all my tears
Smothered the gasping for breath through the years
I've danced with the devil, and still I am here

>   It's mine
>   No, this is the version you get
>
>> *PLATO (handpuppet) joins her.*

LEDA	Plato, constant friend. There you are.
PLATO	I've been with you all the time.
LEDA	I'm sorry I broke your heart. I don't know what I was thinking. I should have let you be a man again Dooley.
PLATO	I once told you that I would do anything to stay with you forever.
LEDA	But Dooley, like this?
PLATO	I don't mind being a monkey.
LEDA	Which is why you're such a good man. Dooley, I'm done. This portrait is complete. Here then are the last snowflakes of my long winter, to rest upon my lashes and freeze my eyes shut.

PLATO	Then curl up my little pink puppy, and sleep.
	Ronnie removes the headrig of LEDA, placing it on the bar. PLATO sings.
	Hold me through this winter day For it's you my blue heart yearns The moon and stars will lead the way Until the sun returns
	The handpuppet of PLATO is removed and rests beside LEDA. Transition. PITY and HERSCHEL are taken from a cabinet.
HERSCHEL	Leaving us so soon, Miss Beane?
PITY	Yes, Mr. Flechtheim. I'm done.
HERSCHEL	You think so?
PITY	I know the provenance of the painting.
HERSCHEL	I've been thinking of this word of yours, my dear. Provenance. My own has a gap of sixty-three years, and while not stolen, it was hidden away. My heart unseen by the one for whom it beat.
PITY	You'll stay then.
HERSCHEL	Indeed. And what of you, my dear? Where will you go now?
PITY	Where I began. Home.
HERSCHEL	Has the thrill of travel worn off so quickly?
PITY	Seeing the world at large has made me feel quite small. And that's really good, Mr. Flechtheim. I don't need to be larger than life.
HERSCHEL	You've come so far to see your boy in the painting. It would be a pity to leave without him. Let me make a gift of it to you, please.
PITY	Thank you for your generosity, Mr. Flechtheim, but no. I have seen him, at last, in the best possible light. So he will be forever real in my mind's eye whenever I need to feel him. But he does not gaze on me, nor should I sit before him in vain, waiting for his breath on my cheek,

	or to speak Pity's name. If I take him with me and return home clinging to him still, then I have not travelled at all. I love him, but I am changed.
HERSCHEL	And what do you desire now, Miss Beane?
PITY	Less. There are so many people in the world. Beauty, the kind you stare at, the kind that makes you lose yourself in your own plainness, that's rare. Which is why it stops you in your tracks. But what about the rest of us, Mr. Flechtheim? Millions of plain people who don't look at each other. If one plain man were to look at me now, I would embrace him. It would scare him, but I would hold onto him. I just want one man to look at me. Just one plain man.
	And not a beauty, please. Not a man who looks at himself in mirrors.
	A plain man, simple. A man who will dance with me. A simple, wrinkled man. I'll be his reflection, and he mine. And we'll dance, plainly. We'll be one another's mirror, but not in vain.
HERSCHEL	I think it would be a shame to leave Vienna without a waltz. Miss Beane.
PITY	Mr. Flechtheim.

HERSCHEL takes PITY in his arms, and they slowly begin to dance. When done, they walk up the ramp together.

HERSCHEL	I know you Canadians think you can walk on frozen water. But be careful, my dear. Something tells me the ice will melt the moment it feels you. I am so glad I lived long enough to meet you.
PITY	Goodbye, Mr. Flechtheim.

She kisses him on the cheek.

There's a freebie. On the house.

HERSCHEL Godspeed, Pity Beane.

HERSCHEL leaves, is put into a cabinet. PITY looks upstage at the painting.

PITY It's unspeakable, this view
Unthinkable loveliness in the plain, simple scene
All I have been cannot compare to this
I am better for finding you and leaving
No farewell glance, no parting kiss
No vow to meet again
You will not notice as I go
So close yet distant still
Look
There are trees in the background

Me in the foreground
Fading from view
But when snowflakes fall, I'll close my eyes
And you'll be there to warm me
Tenderly, as I remember you

> *PITY walks to one of the cabinet doors.*

Goodbye Vienna. You've been a beautiful hostess.

> *PITY is placed in the cabinet, exchanged for another marionette version of her. She is wearing a knitted pink hat and ice skates. The decorative frosted glass around the bottom of the bar is now blue, and she skates in a circle.*

It's unspeakable, this view
There, in the distance
Will familiar trees bend to greet and shade me
We will never meet again, but last in remembrance, fondly

TENDER I have been passed, lonely still life unchanged
But not unmoved. I see too
There is no riddle to solve
No provenance of my own
Please lead me home, as I follow your voice
I am a record of you
There were trees in the background
Me in the foreground
And there, in the distance
This unspeakable view
Beautiful, there you are
All this beauty
All of you

> *PITY continues to skate for a moment, and as the underscore builds she jumps into the air. Lights snap to black.*

> *The end.*

photograph by Helen Tansey

Ronnie Burkett has been captivated by puppetry since the age of seven, when he opened the World Book Encyclopedia to "Puppets." He began touring his puppet shows at the age of fourteen and has been on the road ever since. Ronnie has received numerous awards in Canadian theatre as a playwright, actor and designer for his work with Theatre of Marionettes, and international recognition including a Village Voice OBIE Award in New York for Off-Broadway Theatre. Recognised as one of the world's foremost theatre artists, his work has created an unprecedented adult audience for puppet theatre, and continuously plays to great critical and public acclaim in Canada, the UK, Germany, Australia, Sweden and elsewhere. *Provenance* is the ninth production from Theatre of Marionettes, and follows the now-retired "Memory Dress Trilogy" of *Tinka's New Dress*, *Street of Blood* and *Happy*. Ronnie lives in Toronto.